Drunken
Desserts

Staggeringly Delicious

Sweet temptations

What are drunken desserts? They're delectable pies, brownies, puddings, cobblers and other sweet indulgences that have been nipped and tucked with all kinds of boozy goodness. So kick up your heels and get ready for a totally LUSHious, staggeringly delicious dessert experience!

Printed in China

Published By:

CQProducts

507 Industrial Street
Waverly, IA 50677

ISBN-13: 978-1-56383-398-4
ISBN-10: 1-56383-398-0
Item #7063

Tipsy Tips to Remember

- Make guests aware of the alcoholic ingredients used in each dessert you serve.

- Although heat from baking or simmering reduces the amount of liquor in a cake or sauce, it does not get rid of all of it. The flavor remains, as does some of the alcohol (5 to 85%), so these desserts are not intended for consumption by children and others who wish to avoid alcohol.

Baking with Liquor

- When adding liquor to pudding mixtures and sauces, you may replace some of the liquid in the recipe, but for best results, don't replace all of it.

- To stir liquor into uncooked fillings or frostings, add it in small amounts to maintain correct texture. Taste often! To boost flavor, supplement the liquor with complementary flavored extracts as needed.

- Brush a thin layer of liquor over the surface of cakes, brownies, cookies and crusts to enhance the flavor and kick, but do not over-soak.

- For the biggest buzz, add liquor to heated sauces or liquids *after* they have cooled to room temperature.

Serve up a sweet ending!

Frozen
Strawberry
Margarita Pie

1¼ C. graham cracker crumbs

2 T. sugar

5 T. butter, melted

3½ C. sliced strawberries

1 T. finely grated lime zest

¼ C. lime juice

1 (14 oz.) can sweetened condensed milk

2 T. **tequila**

2 T. **triple sec**

1½ C. heavy whipping cream, chilled

Sliced strawberries and limes, optional

Preheat oven to 350°. Spray a 9″ pie plate (4-cup capacity)* with nonstick cooking spray; set aside. In a medium bowl, stir together graham cracker crumbs, sugar and butter until well mixed. Press mixture evenly in the bottom and up the sides of prepared pie plate. Bake for 10 to 12 minutes or until slightly browned. Let cool in pan about 30 minutes.

Meanwhile, in a blender container, combine sliced strawberries, lime zest, lime juice, sweetened condensed milk, **tequila** and **triple sec**; puree until just smooth. Transfer to a large bowl. In a chilled mixing bowl with chilled beaters, beat whipping cream until it just holds stiff peaks. Gently fold ⅓ of whipped cream into strawberry mixture until blended. Then fold in remaining whipped cream. Pour filling into crust, mounding it slightly. Freeze 4 hours or until firm.

Before serving, remove pie from freezer and let soften in refrigerator about 40 minutes or until semi-soft. Cut into wedges. Garnish with sliced strawberries and limes, if desired.

* A 9″ springform pan can be used. Press crumb mixture in the bottom and 1″ up the sides of pan.

Drunken
Peach Pie Bars

Ingredients

- 2¾ C. flour, divided
- 1½ tsp. salt, divided
- 1 C. vegetable shortening
- 2 eggs, divided
- 7 T. plus 2 tsp. milk, divided
- 1 C. corn flakes cereal
- 1 C. brown sugar
- 2 T. cornstarch
- 1 tsp. ground cinnamon
- 3 to 3½ lbs. ripe peaches, peeled, sliced
- ½ C. plus 2½ T. **peach schnapps**, divided
- 1¾ tsp. almond extract, divided
- ¼ C. coarse sugar
- 1¼ C. powdered sugar, sifted
- 1½ tsp. butter, softened

Serves 12

Preheat oven to 400°. Lightly spray a 9 x 13″ baking pan with nonstick cooking spray; set aside. In a medium bowl, stir together 2½ cups flour and 1 teaspoon salt. With a pastry blender or two knives, cut in shortening until crumbly; set aside. In a small bowl, beat 1 egg yolk (reserve egg white). Add 6 tablespoons plus 2 teaspoons milk and mix well; stir egg mixture into flour mixture until dough forms. On a floured surface, roll half the dough to a 13 x 15″ rectangle. Carefully transfer dough to prepared pan and press firmly in the bottom and up the sides of pan. Sprinkle corn flakes over dough in bottom of pan.

In a large bowl, stir together brown sugar, 2 tablespoons flour, cornstarch, cinnamon and remaining ½ teaspoon salt. Add peaches and mix gently to combine; set aside.

In a separate small bowl, whisk together ½ cup **peach schnapps**, 1 whole egg and 1¼ teaspoons almond extract. Add to peach mixture and stir to combine. Spoon peach mixture into prepared pan. Trim bottom pastry even with the peaches.

On a floured surface, roll remaining dough to a 9 x 13″ rectangle. Transfer dough to prepared pan, covering peach mixture and trimming edges to fit if necessary. Seal together edges of bottom and top pastries using a little water. Cut several small slits in top crust.

Whisk together reserved egg white and remaining 1 tablespoon milk until well blended. Brush top pastry with egg white mixture; sprinkle with coarse sugar.

Bake for 10 to 15 minutes; reduce heat to 375° and bake for 40 minutes more or until pastry is dark golden brown and filling is bubbly. Cool completely. Cut into bars.

In a small bowl, stir together powdered sugar, butter, remaining 2½ tablespoons **peach schnapps** and remaining ½ teaspoon almond extract, adding more **schnapps** if necessary until glaze is thin and smooth. Drizzle over bars as desired.

Grasshopper
Brownies

1 C. butter, softened, divided

1 C. sugar

4 eggs, beaten

1 C. flour

½ tsp. salt

1 (16 oz.) can chocolate syrup

1 tsp. vanilla extract

3 T. crème de menthe, divided

3 T. chocolate cream liqueur, divided

2 C. powdered sugar

½ tsp. mint extract

6 T. heavy whipping cream

1 (11 to 12 oz.) pkg. semi-sweet
    or dark chocolate chips

Preheat oven to 350°. Generously grease a 9 x 13" baking pan; set aside. In a large mixing bowl, beat together ½ cup butter and sugar on medium speed until light and fluffy. Beat in eggs, flour, salt, chocolate syrup and vanilla until well blended. Spread batter in prepared pan and bake for 25 to 30 minutes or until brownies test almost done with a toothpick. Let cool completely.

In a small bowl, stir together 1 tablespoon crème de menthe and 1 tablespoon chocolate liqueur. Brush mixture on brownies; let stand 5 minutes.

Meanwhile, in a medium mixing bowl, beat together remaining ½ cup butter, powdered sugar, remaining 2 tablespoons crème de menthe and mint extract on medium speed until smooth and light. Spread frosting on brownie layer in pan; set aside.

In a medium saucepan over medium-high heat, bring whipping cream to a boil. Remove from heat and add chocolate chips. Let stand for 5 minutes without stirring. Stir until smooth. Stir in remaining 2 tablespoons chocolate liqueur until blended. Cool for 15 minutes. Spread over mint frosting layer. Cover and chill 1 hour or until set. Cut into bars.

crème de **Menthe**

a clear or dark green mint liqueur, excellent drizzled over ice cream, added to recipes and hot beverages or served as an after-dinner drink

Glazed Lush-ious Lemon Cake

Ingredients

2 C. cake flour

1½ tsp. baking powder

½ tsp. salt

1½ C. sugar

½ C. plus 3 T. butter, softened, divided

4 eggs

¾ C. buttermilk

¼ C. plus 3 T. lemon juice, divided

¼ C. plus 5 T. **Limoncello** (lemon liqueur), divided

¼ C. plus 1½ tsp. finely grated lemon zest, divided

¾ C. plus 6 T. powdered sugar, sifted, divided

1 pt. fresh blueberries

Spray whipped topping (such as Reddi-wip)

Serves 10

Preheat oven to 350°. Spray a 9 x 13″ baking pan with nonstick cooking spray; set aside. In a medium bowl, sift together flour, baking powder and salt; set aside. In a large mixing bowl, combine sugar and ½ cup butter. Beat on medium speed until light and fluffy. Add eggs, one at a time, beating well after each addition. Add flour mixture and buttermilk alternately to the butter mixture until blended. Beat in ¼ cup lemon juice, ¼ cup **Limoncello** and ¼ cup lemon zest. Spread batter in prepared pan and bake for 25 to 30 minutes or until cake tests done with a toothpick. Cool completely. Brush top of cake with 2 tablespoons **Limoncello**.

In a small saucepan over low heat, combine remaining 3 tablespoons butter, ¾ cup powdered sugar and remaining 3 tablespoons lemon juice, 3 tablespoons **Limoncello** and 1½ teaspoons lemon zest. Stir until butter melts and mixture comes to a simmer. Whisk in additional powdered sugar, by tablespoonful, until glaze reaches desired drizzling consistency.

To assemble dessert, cut cake into small cubes. Arrange a layer of cubes in each dessert dish and sprinkle with a few blueberries. Spoon half of warm glaze over cake and berries. Add another layer of cake cubes, blueberries and remaining glaze. Just before serving, add a swirl of whipped topping.

Limoncello

Also known as lemon liqueur, it's a classic after-dinner drink, with or without ice. Try it on ice cream or in fruit salad too.

Strawberry *Tipsy* Torte

Ingredients

- ⅔ C. flour
- 3 T. finely chopped pecans
- 2 T. brown sugar
- ⅓ C. butter, softened
- 1 (8 oz.) pkg. cream cheese, softened
- 1 C. milk
- ⅓ C. **light rum**
- 1 (3.4 oz.) pkg. lemon instant pudding mix
- 3 C. sliced fresh strawberries, plus 1 whole berry
- 1 (3 oz.) pkg. strawberry gelatin
- ¼ C. **triple sec**

Preheat oven to 350°. In a medium bowl, stir together flour, pecans and brown sugar. With a pastry blender or two knives, cut in butter until crumbly. Press mixture in the bottom of an ungreased 9″ springform pan. Bake for 15 to 20 minutes or until lightly browned. Let cool completely.

In a medium mixing bowl, beat cream cheese on medium speed until smooth and creamy. Slowly blend in milk. Mix in **rum**. Add pudding mix and beat on low speed for 1 minute or until thickened. Pour over cooled crust, spreading evenly. Arrange sliced strawberries in a circular pattern on top of pudding layer as desired, starting around outer edge. Cut berries into smaller pieces as needed. Place whole berry in the middle, pointed side up. Refrigerate while preparing topping.

In a large microwave-safe measuring cup, bring ¾ cup water to a boil. Add gelatin and stir until completely dissolved, about 2 minutes. Stir in ½ cup cold water and **triple sec** until blended. Slowly pour gelatin mixture over strawberries. Refrigerate at least 3 hours or until set.

To serve, loosen filling from side of pan with a knife dipped in hot water. Carefully remove side of pan and slice into wedges.

Buzzed
Brandy Snaps

Ingredients

- ¼ C. butter
- ¼ C. molasses
- 2 T. sugar
- 2 T. brown sugar
- ½ C. flour
- ¼ tsp. ground ginger
- Pinch of salt
- 1 T. brandy*, divided
- 1½ C. heavy whipping cream
- 3 T. powdered sugar
- 2 T. finely chopped dark chocolate chips
- 6 wood dowels (6″ long, 1″ diameter)

Serves 12

Preheat oven to 350°. Line a baking sheet with parchment paper; set aside. In a medium saucepan over medium heat, combine butter, molasses, sugar and brown sugar, stirring constantly until butter melts. Simmer for 30 seconds. Remove from heat; stir in flour, ginger and salt, mixing until smooth. Stir in 1½ teaspoons brandy.

Working in batches, drop heaping teaspoonfuls of batter on prepared baking sheet, leaving about 4″ between cookies. Bake for 8 to 10 minutes or until cookies are flattened and lacy.

Meanwhile, wrap each dowel piece in waxed paper, parchment paper or smooth aluminum foil; set aside.

Cool cookies on baking sheet until you can easily lift them with a metal spatula without wrinkling the cookies. Immediately wrap each cookie around a covered dowel piece and set cookies, seam side down, on a wire cooling rack until completely cooled. When cool, slide cookies off dowels. Repeat with remaining batter.

In a chilled medium bowl with chilled beaters, beat whipping cream, powdered sugar and remaining 1½ teaspoons brandy on high speed until stiff peaks form. Pipe whipped cream mixture into each cookie and sprinkle chopped chocolate chips on the ends of each. Serve immediately.

* Using bourbon is also delicious.

Brandy **Snaps**

popular treats at old English fairs,
though they were often flat, not rolled

Pear *Martini* Crisp

Ingredients

- ⅓ C. plus 2 T. **pear** or **vanilla vodka**, divided
- 1 T. lemon juice
- 2 tsp. ground cinnamon, plus more for sprinkling, divided
- ¼ tsp. ground nutmeg
- 1¼ C. plus ⅔ C. brown sugar, divided
- 4½ C. fresh pears, peeled, cored, sliced
- ⅔ C. flour
- ⅔ C. coarsely chopped walnuts
- ⅓ C. plus 3 T. butter, divided
- 1½ tsp. light corn syrup
- 1 C. heavy whipping cream
- 2 T. sugar

Preheat oven to 350°. Spray an 8″ round cake pan or 9″ pie plate with non-stick cooking spray; set aside. In a medium bowl, stir together ⅓ cup **vodka**, lemon juice, 2 teaspoons cinnamon, nutmeg and ¼ cup brown sugar. Measure 1½ tablespoons of vodka mixture into a small bowl; set aside. To remaining vodka mixture in medium bowl, add pears and toss until fruit is completely glazed. Pour mixture into prepared pan; set aside.

In a medium microwave-safe bowl, melt ⅓ cup butter. Stir in flour, walnuts and ⅔ cup brown sugar until well combined and crumbly. Sprinkle mixture evenly over pears.

Bake for 35 to 40 minutes or until topping is golden brown and filling is bubbly. Remove from oven and let cool.

In a small saucepan over medium heat, combine remaining 3 tablespoons butter and remaining 1 cup brown sugar. Boil for about 5 minutes, stirring constantly until smooth. Remove from heat and stir in corn syrup. Cool caramel sauce for 15 minutes. Add set-aside vodka mixture and stir well.

In a chilled medium mixing bowl with chilled beaters, beat whipping cream and sugar on high speed until stiff peaks form. Stir in remaining 2 tablespoons **vodka**.

To serve, spoon pear crisp into individual serving bowls. Top with caramel sauce and whipped cream. Sprinkle lightly with cinnamon, if desired.

pear**Vodka**

a flavored vodka, perfect chilled and straight up in a classic martini

Toasted Piña Colada Pie

½ C. sweetened flaked coconut, toasted*, divided

¼ C. sliced almonds, toasted*

1¼ C. graham cracker crumbs

2 T. sugar

⅓ C. butter, melted

1 (3 oz.) pkg. island pineapple gelatin

4 oz. cream cheese, softened

1 (8 oz.) can crushed pineapple

3 T. coconut rum

2 C. whipped topping, divided

Serves 8

Preheat oven to 350°. Crush ¼ cup toasted coconut and set aside. Coarsely break up 2 tablespoons toasted almonds and reserve for later use. Spray a 9″ pie plate (4-cup capacity) with nonstick cooking spray; set aside. In a medium bowl, stir together graham cracker crumbs, sugar, butter and crushed coconut until well mixed. Press mixture evenly in the bottom and up the sides of prepared pie plate. Bake for 10 to 12 minutes or until slightly browned. Let cool in pan for 30 minutes.

Meanwhile, in a large microwave-safe measuring cup, bring ⅔ cup water to a boil. Add gelatin and stir until completely dissolved, about 2 minutes; set aside. In a medium mixing bowl, beat cream cheese on medium speed until creamy. Gradually beat in gelatin mixture. Whisk in pineapple, coconut rum and 1 cup whipped topping until thoroughly blended. Sprinkle reserved broken almonds over graham cracker crust. Spread cream cheese filling evenly in crust. Refrigerate 3 hours or overnight.

Before serving, cut into wedges and top with dollops of remaining whipped topping. Garnish with remaining toasted coconut and almonds.

* To toast, place coconut and almonds on separate baking sheets in a 350° oven for about 10 minutes or until evenly browned, stirring occasionally.

Twisted Ice Cream Tiramisu

Ingredients

1½ (3.5 oz.) pkgs. ladyfingers
(32 to 36 cookies)

¼ C. brewed coffee, room temperature

¼ C. **Kahlúa** (coffee liqueur)

1 pt. coffee ice cream, softened

3 (1 oz.) squares bittersweet chocolate,
grated or finely chopped, divided

3 C. whipped topping, divided

1 pt. dulce de leche ice cream

1 T. **caramel cream liqueur**

Milk chocolate curls, optional

Directions

Line an 8″ square baking pan with aluminum foil, leaving a 2″ overhang on two opposite sides; spray with nonstick cooking spray. Arrange half the ladyfingers in the bottom of pan to cover; set aside. In a small bowl, stir together coffee and **Kahlúa**. Brush half of coffee mixture over ladyfingers in pan, allowing mixture to soak in. Stir coffee ice cream until smooth but not melted; spread over ladyfingers. Sprinkle half of grated chocolate over ice cream. Dollop 1½ cups whipped topping over chocolate and spread evenly. Place in freezer for at least 30 minutes or until firm.

To make second layer, soften dulce de leche ice cream in a medium bowl. Arrange remaining ladyfingers over whipped topping. Brush cookies with remaining coffee mixture. Stir **caramel liqueur** into softened ice cream and spread mixture over ladyfingers. Sprinkle remaining chocolate over ice cream. Dollop remaining whipped topping over chocolate layer and spread until smooth. Cover and freeze at least 3 hours or overnight.

Thirty minutes before serving, place dessert in refrigerator to soften slightly. Remove dessert from pan, peel off foil and cut into squares. Garnish with chocolate curls.

Liqueurs

Also known as cordials, they're thicker and smoother than other alcoholic beverages and are usually served as after–dinner drinks, poured over ice cream or used in desserts.

Party Time
Sangria

1 (3 oz.) pkg. strawberry gelatin

1 (3 oz.) pkg. lemon gelatin

1 C. **dry red wine**

8 fresh strawberries

1 (11 oz.) can mandarin orange segments

1 C. seedless red grapes

Serves 4

In a medium bowl, combine strawberry and lemon gelatin. Add 1½ cups boiling water, stirring for 2 minutes or until completely dissolved.

In a 2-cup measuring cup, combine **wine** with enough ice cubes to measure 1½ cups. Add to gelatin mixture, stirring until ice melts and gelatin is slightly thickened (or refrigerate 10 to 15 minutes to thicken slightly, removing any unmelted ice).

Slice strawberries and drain mandarin oranges. Cut grapes in half, if desired. Divide fruit evenly between four 12- to 18-ounce clear glass dessert dishes or wine glasses.

Pour gelatin mixture evenly over fruit in glasses, stirring carefully to distribute fruit. Refrigerate 4 hours or until firm.

Sangria

Typically known as a party punch,, it can be changed up in any number of ways. The common elements are fruit and wine, but other ingredients such as fruit juice, carbonated soda and other alcohol can be added.

Spiked
Eggnog
Cream Puffs

Ingredients

½ C. butter

1 C. flour

4 eggs, lightly beaten

1 (3.4 oz.) pkg. vanilla instant pudding mix

½ C. milk

⅓ C. **light rum** (or less to taste)

1 tsp. ground nutmeg

¼ tsp. ground ginger

1¼ C. heavy whipping cream

Powdered sugar

Preheat oven to 400°. In a medium saucepan over medium-high heat, combine 1 cup water and butter. Bring mixture to a rolling boil. Reduce heat to low and stir in flour, beating vigorously until mixture forms a ball, about 1 minute. Remove from heat and let stand for 1 to 2 minutes. Beat in eggs all at once, whisking until smooth. Drop dough onto ungreased baking sheet by scant ¼ cupfuls, placing puffs about 3" apart. Bake for 35 to 40 minutes or until puffed and golden brown. Cool completely on baking sheets.

Meanwhile, in a medium mixing bowl, beat together pudding mix, milk, **rum**, nutmeg and ginger on medium speed until well blended, about 1 minute. Add whipping cream and beat on high speed until soft peaks form, about 2 minutes. Cover and chill at least 30 minutes or until needed.

To assemble, cut off tops of cooled puffs and pull out any filaments of soft dough. Spoon or pipe chilled filling into the bottom half of each puff and replace top. Serve immediately or cover and refrigerate no longer than 3 hours. Just before serving, sprinkle with powdered sugar.

variation

To substitute spiced rum in the filling, use ¾ cup milk and ¼ cup spiced rum plus other ingredients as listed.

Loaded
Sandwich
Cookies

Ingredients

1 (18.25 oz.) pkg. dark chocolate
    cake mix (pudding type)

½ C. butter, melted

1 egg, slightly beaten

Creamy Filling (choose Peanut Butter,
    Raspberry or Peppermint;
    recipes on opposite page)

Serves 12

Preheat oven to 350°. In a large bowl, combine cake mix, butter and egg. Mix well with a spoon. Firmly shape dough into 1¼″ balls. (You'll need two balls for each sandwich cookie.) Place balls 2″ apart on ungreased baking sheets. Bake for 10 to 13 minutes or until set and cracked on top. Cool cookies on baking sheet for 1 minute before removing to a wire rack to cool completely.

Prepare one of the fillings below. Pipe or spread chilled filling on the flat side of half the cookies; top with remaining cookies. Refrigerate until serving.

Peanut Butter

In a medium bowl, beat together 4 ounces softened cream cheese, 6 tablespoons creamy peanut butter and ½ teaspoon vanilla on medium speed until creamy. Beat in 2 cups powdered sugar. Stir in 3 tablespoons Frangelico until blended. Beat in ½ cup additional powdered sugar. Chill for 30 minutes.

Raspberry

In a medium bowl, beat together 4 ounces softened cream cheese, 6 tablespoons softened butter and ½ teaspoon vanilla on medium speed until creamy. Beat in 2 cups powdered sugar. Stir in 3 tablespoons raspberry schnapps and 2 to 3 tablespoons seedless raspberry preserves until blended. Beat in ½ cup additional powdered sugar. Tint with red food coloring as desired. Chill for 30 minutes.

Peppermint

In a medium bowl, beat together 4 ounces softened cream cheese, 6 tablespoons softened butter and ½ teaspoon vanilla on medium speed until creamy. Beat in 2 cups powdered sugar. Stir in 3 tablespoons peppermint schnapps and ¼ teaspoon peppermint extract until blended. Beat in ½ cup additional powdered sugar. Chill for 30 minutes.

Boozy
Brownie
Swirls

Ingredients

1 (18 to 20 oz.) pkg. brownie mix

Vegetable oil and eggs as directed on
 brownie mix package

¼ C. stout beer

1 (8 oz.) pkg. cream cheese, softened

⅓ C. sugar

1 egg

2 T. Irish cream

Preheat oven to 350°. Spray nine 6-ounce ramekins or a muffin pan with nonstick cooking spray; set aside. In a large mixing bowl, combine brownie mix with oil and eggs as directed on package, stirring in beer in place of water. Divide batter evenly among prepared ramekins; set aside.

In a medium mixing bowl, beat together cream cheese and sugar on medium speed until well combined and creamy. Beat in egg until thoroughly mixed. Stir in Irish cream. Spoon mixture evenly over brownie batter in ramekins. Using a fork or knife, gently swirl mixtures.

Set ramekins on a baking sheet and bake for 35 to 40 minutes or until the middle is just set and small cracks begin to form. Cool completely.

Stout**Beer**

has a deep dark color and bittersweet flavor. To pour, angle a glass to 45° and fill ¾ full. Then let it settle before pouring to fill the glass. Voilà! The perfect head of white foam!

Blitzed
Boston
Cream

Ingredients

1 (18.25 oz.) pkg. yellow cake mix

Water, vegetable oil and eggs as directed
    on cake mix package

1 (3.9 oz.) pkg. chocolate instant pudding mix

1 C. powdered sugar, divided

3 C. milk, divided

½ C. **chocolate cream liqueur**

1 (3.4 oz.) pkg. vanilla instant pudding mix

½ C. **Irish cream**

Whipped topping

Grated chocolate, optional

Serves 12

Preheat oven to 350°. Grease and flour a 9 x 13" baking pan; set aside. In a large mixing bowl, combine cake mix with water, oil and eggs as directed on package. Spread batter in prepared pan and bake according to package instructions for pan size. Remove cake from oven. Using the round handle of a wooden spoon, poke holes through top of warm cake at 1" intervals without piercing all the way through; set aside.

In a medium bowl, stir together chocolate pudding mix, ½ cup powdered sugar and 1½ cups milk; whisk for 1 minute until well blended. Do not over-mix. Stir in **chocolate liqueur** just until blended. Pour the thin pudding mixture slowly and evenly over the warm cake, letting it run into the holes to make stripes in the cake. Refrigerate 30 minutes.

Meanwhile, in a medium bowl, stir together vanilla pudding mix, remaining ½ cup powdered sugar and remaining 1½ cups milk; whisk for 1 minute until well blended. Do not over-mix. Stir in **Irish cream** just until blended. Let mixture stand for 15 minutes until slightly thickened. Spread vanilla pudding mixture evenly over chocolate layer. Refrigerate at least 1 hour before serving. Cut into squares and garnish with dollops of whipped topping and grated chocolate.

IrishCream

Irish whiskey, cream and fine spirits woven together

Rum-Spiked
Cherry Cobbler

¼ C. plus 6 T. butter, divided

7 T. brown sugar, divided

2 (12 oz.) bags frozen dark sweet cherries

¼ C. plus 2 T. **light rum**, divided

1 T. plus 2 tsp. cornstarch, divided

¼ tsp. ground cinnamon

1⅓ C. flour

2 T. sugar

1 tsp. baking powder

⅛ tsp. salt

¼ C. heavy whipping cream,
    plus more for brushing

¼ C. coarse sugar

¼ tsp. almond extract

Preheat oven to 375°. Lightly spray four 8-ounce ramekins with cooking spray; set aside. In a large skillet over medium heat, melt ¼ cup butter. Add 3 tablespoons brown sugar, stirring to combine. Add cherries and ¼ cup **rum**. Cook, stirring frequently, about 5 minutes. Using a slotted spoon, transfer cherries to a large bowl; reserve juice in skillet.

To cherries in bowl, add 2 tablespoons brown sugar, 1 tablespoon cornstarch and cinnamon. Mix well to evenly coat cherries; set aside.

In a medium bowl, stir together flour, sugar, remaining 2 tablespoons brown sugar, baking powder and salt. Cut remaining 6 tablespoons butter into small pieces. Add to flour mixture and combine with a pastry blender or two knives until mixture resembles coarse crumbs. Add ¼ cup whipping cream and mix just until dough comes together in a ball.

Place prepared ramekins on a baking sheet. Divide cherries evenly between ramekins and bake for about 5 minutes or just until heated through. Remove from oven and drop pieces of dough over warm cherries. Brush dough with a little whipping cream and sprinkle with coarse sugar. Return to oven and bake for 20 to 25 minutes or until topping is golden brown and filling is bubbly. Remove from oven.

In a small bowl, stir together remaining 2 teaspoons cornstarch and 1 tablespoon cold water, stirring until cornstarch is dissolved and mixture is smooth. Add to reserved juice in skillet. Stir in almond extract. Cook and stir over medium-low heat until slightly thickened. Remove from heat and cool slightly. Stir in remaining 2 tablespoons **rum** and serve with cobbler.

Punchy Crunchy
Pecan Pie

Ingredients

- 1½ C. flour
- ½ C. vegetable shortening
- ¾ tsp. salt, divided
- 3 to 3½ T. milk
- 6 eggs
- 1 C. ground pecans
- ½ C. plus 1 T. **bourbon**, divided
- 2 C. plus 1 tsp. sugar, divided
- ¼ C. melted butter
- 1 C. chopped pecans, toasted*
- 1 C. plus 8 whole pecans, toasted*, divided
- 1 C. heavy whipping cream

Serves 8

Preheat oven to 350°. Lightly spray a 10″ pie plate with nonstick cooking spray; set aside. In a medium bowl, combine flour, shortening and ½ teaspoon salt, using a pastry blender or two knives to blend together until fine crumbs form. Stir in milk, a little at a time, until dough begins to hold together, but isn't sticky. On a floured surface, roll dough into a 13″ circle, about ¼″ thick. Carefully transfer dough to prepared pie plate**, pressing gently, without stretching, in the bottom and up the sides of plate. Trim off excess dough and flute edges. Place in freezer while making filling.

In a medium bowl, whisk eggs until frothy. Add ground pecans, ½ cup **bourbon**, 2 cups sugar, butter and remaining ¼ teaspoon salt, mixing to combine thoroughly. Stir in chopped pecans and 1 cup whole pecans.

Remove pie crust from freezer and pour filling mixture into crust. Place pie on a baking sheet. Bake for 45 to 65 minutes or until crust is golden brown and center of filling is slightly puffed. Filling may be slightly soft in the center. Remove pie from baking sheet and cool completely. Refrigerate several hours before cutting into wedges.

In a small bowl, beat whipping cream and remaining 1 teaspoon sugar until soft peaks form. Add remaining 1 tablespoon **bourbon** and beat until stiff peaks form. Top pie with dollops of whipped cream and garnish with remaining whole pecans. Serve promptly.

 * To toast, place pecans on a baking sheet in a 350° oven for about 10 minutes or until evenly browned, stirring occasionally.

** After rolling dough, carefully fold in half and remove from the work surface using a large metal spatula. Place in the center of prepared pan and unfold.

Serves 12

Drunkerita
Caketail

Ingredients

1 (18.25 oz.) pkg. white cake mix

Water, vegetable oil and egg whites as directed on cake mix package

1 T. plus ⅓ C. **tequila**, divided

3 C. prepared creamy white decorator icing, room temperature, divided

1 (3 oz.) pkg. lime gelatin

Coarse sugar

Lime slices, optional

Preheat oven to 350°. Spray two 8″ round baking pans with nonstick cooking spray and line bottoms with parchment paper. Spray again and set aside. In a large mixing bowl, combine cake mix with water, oil and egg whites as directed on package. Divide batter between prepared pans and bake according to package instructions for pan size. Cool in pans for 15 minutes. Remove cakes from pans to cool completely.

With a serrated knife, trim off crowned area on cake tops as needed to create a flat surface. Place one cake on a serving platter and brush top with 1 tablespoon **tequila**; spread with about 1 cup icing. Set second cake layer over icing, edges even. Spread icing on side of cake. Cut and remove a disk of cake from the top layer to make a "pool" about ¾″ deep with a 1″ rim. *(If desired, use a 6″ bowl as a pattern.)* Reserve removed cake for another use. Spread more icing over top rim of cake. In a microwave-safe bowl, warm ½ cup icing for 10 seconds to thin; stir well. Spread thinned icing over cut area of cake to seal. Refrigerate at least 10 minutes.

Meanwhile, in a medium bowl, combine gelatin with ¾ cup boiling water; stir until completely dissolved. In a 2-cup measuring cup, combine remaining ⅓ cup **tequila** with enough ice cubes to make 1¼ cups. Stir ice mixture into gelatin until slightly thickened; remove any unmelted ice. Ladle gelatin mixture into "pool" until level with top. (You may have extra gelatin.) Place ⅓ cup icing into a piping bag fitted with a small round tip. Pipe small dots around the upper edge of gelatin. Switch to a large round tip and pipe large dots around the base of cake. Sprinkle coarse sugar around upper edge of cake. Refrigerate 4 hours or overnight. If desired, garnish with lime slices and drinking straws before serving.

Boozed-Up
Banana
Trifle

Ingredients

2 T. plus ½ C. light rum, divided

3 T. bourbon, divided

1 (12 oz. box) vanilla wafers
(there will be extras)

7 C. milk

4 (3 oz.) pkgs. vanilla cook–and–serve
pudding mix

8 bananas

1½ C. milk chocolate toffee bits

1 C. heavy whipping cream

1 T. sugar

Serves 12

In a small bowl, mix 2 tablespoons rum and 2 tablespoons bourbon. Arrange 50 to 60 vanilla wafers on a rimmed baking sheet and brush lightly with rum mixture; set aside.

In a large saucepan over medium-low heat, combine milk with pudding mixes, whisking to blend well. Cook, stirring constantly, until mixture thickens and comes to a full boil. Remove from heat. Place plastic wrap on surface of pudding; let cool for 10 minutes before whisking in remaining ½ cup rum. Refrigerate until assembly.

Peel and slice bananas. To assemble trifle, arrange about ⅓ of the prepared wafers in the bottom and up the sides of a deep 2½-quart glass bowl. Place about ⅓ of the sliced bananas over wafers and against side of bowl. Spread ⅓ of the pudding mixture over bananas. Sprinkle ⅓ of the toffee bits generously around edge of bowl and over top of pudding. Repeat with two more layers of wafers, bananas, pudding and toffee bits. Refrigerate at least 1 hour.

In a chilled bowl with chilled beaters, beat whipping cream with sugar until soft peaks form. Stir in remaining 1 tablespoon bourbon. Before serving, place dollops of whipped cream on trifle and garnish with plain wafers as desired.

variation

Instead of pudding mix, make a large batch of your favorite homemade vanilla pudding.

Boozy–Woozy
Chocolate-
Raspberry
Cups

1½ C. semi–sweet chocolate chips

3 T. butter

3 to 4 tsp. vegetable shortening

1 C. heavy whipping cream

¾ C. chocolate syrup

2 T. **raspberry schnapps**

Line 15 mini muffin cups with paper liners; set aside. In a microwave-safe bowl, melt chocolate chips, stirring until smooth. Add butter and shortening; stir until melted and smooth. Spoon 1 tablespoon of melted mixture into a paper liner. With a small paintbrush, coat the inside of liner with a layer of chocolate, from bottom toward top edge. Repeat to make additional cups. Chill until set. Brush on a second layer of chocolate and refrigerate until set. Before using, gently peel off paper liners and refrigerate chocolate cups until ready to use.

In a small chilled mixing bowl with chilled beaters, beat whipping cream on high speed until stiff peaks form. Stir in chocolate syrup and **raspberry schnapps** until well combined. Spoon mixture into chocolate cups and freeze for several hours. Serve immediately after removing from freezer. These treats do not freeze solid.

variation

For the chocoholic, make these desserts in six standard muffin cups for an intense chocolate treat.

raspberrySchnapps

Serve with ice cream, cheese and cheese cakes, or use it in jams, marmalades and sauces. Also excellent as a drink before or after dinner.

Tiny Tequila Sunsets

Ingredients

1 (3 oz.) pkg. tropical fusion gelatin

¼ C. **blackberry brandy**

1 (3 oz.) pkg. orange gelatin

¼ C. **tequila**

1 tsp. finely grated orange zest

1 C. whipped topping

Fresh orange peel, optional

Maraschino cherries, optional

Serves 9

Place tropical fusion gelatin in a medium bowl and add 1 cup boiling water, stirring for 2 minutes or until completely dissolved. Stir in ¼ cup cold water; let mixture stand for 5 to 10 minutes to cool slightly. Stir in **blackberry brandy**. Pour mixture into an 8″ square pan and refrigerate at least 1½ hours or until set.

Place orange gelatin in a medium bowl and add 1 cup boiling water, stirring for 2 minutes or until completely dissolved. Let stand for 5 to 10 minutes to cool slightly. Stir in **tequila** and orange zest. Add whipped topping and mix until well blended. Pour mixture over first layer of gelatin in pan. Refrigerate at least 3 hours or until firm. Cut into small squares and garnish with orange curls* and skewered cherries, if desired.

* To make orange peel curls, cut long thin strips of peel (without pith) and wrap around a plastic drinking straw. Let dry.

Blackberry**Brandy**

Enjoy it at room temperature in a brandy snifter as an after-dinner drink or mixed in a cocktail.

Mudsicle
Squares

Ingredients

2¼ C. cream-filled chocolate cookie crumbs

¾ C. ground pecans, divided

4½ T. **Kahlúa** (coffee liqueur), divided

¼ C. melted butter

2 (8 oz.) pkgs. cream cheese, softened

1 (14 oz.) can sweetened condensed milk

¾ C. chocolate syrup, divided

1 (8 oz.) container whipped topping, divided

¼ C. milk

In a small bowl, stir together cookie crumbs, ½ cup pecans, 1 tablespoon **Kahlúa** and butter. Press in the bottom of a 9 x 13″ baking pan; set aside.

In a large mixing bowl, beat cream cheese on medium speed until light and fluffy. Blend in 1½ tablespoons **Kahlúa**, sweetened condensed milk and ½ cup chocolate syrup. Set aside ½ cup whipped topping. Blend remaining whipped topping into chocolate mixture; spread over crust. Cover and freeze overnight before cutting into squares.

In a small bowl, stir together milk, remaining ¼ cup chocolate syrup, remaining 2 tablespoons **Kahlúa** and reserved ½ cup whipped topping; drizzle over dessert squares. Sprinkle with remaining pecans before serving.

coffeeLiqueur

Made from sugarcane and coffee, it also comes in several different flavors such as French vanilla and mocha. Serve it over ice in a cocktail glass or stir it into a cold or hot drink.

Grown-Up S'mores

½ C. brewed coffee, cooled
¼ C. **Frangelico** (hazelnut liqueur)*
12 graham cracker squares
16 regular-sized marshmallows
3 (1.55 oz.) milk chocolate candy bars

Serves 4

Preheat oven to 375°. Spray four 8-ounce ramekins with nonstick cooking spray; set aside. In a shallow bowl, stir together coffee and **Frangelico**. Break graham crackers into pieces to fit ramekins. Dip both sides of a few graham cracker pieces into coffee mixture and arrange in a single layer in the bottom of each ramekin. Top each with ¼ of a candy bar.

Using kitchen shears dipped in water, cut each marshmallow into four crosswise slices and place four or five slices on each candy bar piece. Repeat layers two times until ramekins are full. Reserve remaining coffee mixture.

Set ramekins on a baking sheet. Bake for 12 to 15 minutes or until chocolate is soft and top marshmallow pieces are toasty brown. Remove from oven and drizzle about 1 tablespoon coffee mixture over each ramekin. Serve warm.

* Amaretto also tastes delicious.

Amaretto

a unique almond-flavored liqueur to appreciate straight up, on the rocks or in an array of cocktails

Frangelico

a hazelnut liqueur that's perfect after a meal – over ice, with coffee or in coffee

Black Forest
Brownies

Ingredients

1 (18.3 oz.) pkg. fudge brownie mix

Water, vegetable oil and egg as directed on brownie mix package

1 (21 oz.) can cherry pie filling

¼ C. **cherry brandy**, divided

1 tsp. almond extract, divided

2 C. heavy whipping cream

½ C. powdered sugar

Preheat oven to 350°. Lightly spray two 8″ round baking pans with nonstick cooking spray. Line bottom of pans with parchment paper and spray again; set aside. Combine brownie mix with water, oil and egg as directed on package. Divide batter between prepared pans and bake as directed for a 9x13″ pan. Cool completely.

In a small bowl, stir together pie filling, 1 tablespoon **cherry brandy** and ½ teaspoon almond extract; set aside.

In a medium chilled mixing bowl with chilled beaters, beat whipping cream until frothy. Gradually beat in powdered sugar on high speed until stiff peaks form. Stir in remaining ½ teaspoon almond extract and 1 tablespoon **cherry brandy**.

Remove brownies from pan and peel off parchment paper. Trim edge of one brownie as needed to fit the bottom of an 8″ round dessert dish (2½ to 3 quarts)*, using removed parchment paper as a guide. Place brownie in dish. Brush top of brownie with 1 tablespoon **cherry brandy**. Reserve about 12 whole cherries from pie filling; spoon remaining pie filling over brownie. Spread half of whipped cream over cherry layer. Trim remaining brownie as needed to fit next layer in dessert dish; set brownie on top of whipped cream layer. Brush top of brownie with remaining 1 tablespoon **cherry brandy**. Top with remaining whipped cream. Cut trimmed brownies into small cubes. Garnish dessert with reserved cherries and brownie cubes as desired.

* Or, simply cut each brownie into 1″ pieces, layer pieces in the dish and drizzle with cherry brandy while assembling layers as directed.

Jammin' Vanilla Cheesecake

Ingredients

⅓ C. vegetable shortening

3 T. brown sugar

⅔ C. flour

½ C. quick-cooking oats

⅛ tsp. salt

½ C. seedless raspberry preserves

5 T. **vanilla vodka**, divided

7½ tsp. vanilla extract, divided

½ tsp. unflavored gelatin

2 (8 oz.) pkgs. cream cheese, softened

⅔ C. plus ¼ C. sugar, divided

6 T. heavy whipping cream

2 C. frozen raspberries, thawed

Serves 9

Preheat oven to 350°. Spray an 8˝ square baking pan with nonstick cooking spray; set aside. In a medium bowl, combine shortening and brown sugar; mix with a spoon until creamy and well blended. Add flour, oats and salt, mixing thoroughly until crumbly. Press dough in prepared pan. Bake for 15 to 17 minutes or until golden brown. Let cool completely.

In a small bowl, whisk together preserves and 2 teaspoons **vanilla vodka**. Spread over cooled crust and set aside.

In a small saucepan, combine 8 teaspoons **vanilla vodka** and 4 teaspoons vanilla. Sprinkle gelatin over mixture and let stand for 10 minutes. Place saucepan over low heat and stir just until dissolved. Cool to barely lukewarm. Meanwhile, in a large mixing bowl, combine cream cheese, ²/₃ cup sugar and 1½ teaspoons vanilla. Beat at medium speed until smooth and creamy. Beat in whipping cream. Add gelatin mixture and beat until blended. Spread cream cheese mixture over preserves. Cover and refrigerate 5 hours or overnight.

In a small bowl, combine raspberries with remaining 5 teaspoons **vanilla vodka**, 2 teaspoons vanilla and ¼ cup sugar. Let stand 15 minutes. To serve, cut dessert into squares and top with raspberry mixture.

Poked

Cake Shots

Ingredients

1 (18.25 oz.) pkg. white cake mix

Water, vegetable oil and egg whites as
  directed on cake mix package

3 (3 oz.) pkgs. raspberry gelatin

½ C. plus 1 T. **raspberry schnapps**

3 T. **crème de almond liqueur**

Whipped topping

Colored sprinkles, optional

* Number of servings depends
  on size of containers used.

Preheat oven to 350°. Spray bottom of a 12 x 18″ jelly roll pan with nonstick cooking spray; set aside. In a large mixing bowl, combine cake mix with water, oil and egg whites as directed on package. Spread batter in prepared pan and bake for 12 to 15 minutes or until cake tests done with a toothpick. Cool cake in pan for 15 minutes. With a large fork, poke cake at ½″ intervals without piercing all the way through.

Place gelatin in a medium bowl and add 3 cups boiling water, stirring for 2 minutes or until completely dissolved. Stir in ¾ cup cold water, **raspberry schnapps** and **almond liqueur** until blended. Pour 1 to 1½ cups of gelatin mixture over cake, allowing it to soak into holes. Refrigerate 3 hours.

Pour remaining gelatin mixture into small dessert dishes or shot glasses (2- to 4-ounce capacity), filling each one halfway. Refrigerate until set.

To assemble, use a round cookie cutter that matches the size of dessert dishes or shot glasses being used**. Spray cutter lightly with nonstick cooking spray; cut one round of chilled cake for each dessert. Carefully set cake round over gelatin layer in each dish or glass, pressing gently until cake rests on gelatin. Refrigerate until serving time. Top with whipped topping and colored sprinkles, if desired.

** You may also cut out cake rounds using a drinking glass lightly sprayed with nonstick cooking spray.

Great flavor combos:

Lime gelatin + vanilla vodka or lime vodka
Berry Blue gelatin + blue curaçao
Peach gelatin + peach schnapps
Tropical Fusion gelatin + light rum
Cherry gelatin + cherry brandy
(Use 3 packages of gelatin with ¾ cup alcohol and water as directed above.)

Schnapp–y
Chocolate
Cake Balls

Ingredients

1 (18.25 oz.) pkg. chocolate cake mix

Water, vegetable oil and eggs as directed
  on cake mix package

15 mint Oreo cookies, crushed (about 2 C.)

¾ to 1 C. peppermint schnapps

2 (12 oz.) pkgs. milk chocolate chips

1 (4.67 oz.) pkg. Andes crème de menthe
  candies (about 28), chopped, divided

Serves 50

Preheat oven to 350°. Spray a 9 x 13″ baking pan with nonstick cooking spray; set aside. In a large mixing bowl, combine cake mix with water, oil and eggs as directed on package. Spread batter in prepared pan and bake according to package instructions for pan size. Let cool completely.

Cut cake into pieces and use hands to crumble the cake into a large bowl. Add crushed Oreos and mix well with a spoon. Stir in peppermint schnapps, a little at a time, until mixture holds together like thick moist dough. Cover bowl and refrigerate at least 2 hours or overnight.

Line a baking sheet with waxed paper. Form dough into small firm balls, 1″ to 1½″ in diameter. Place on prepared baking sheet and freeze at least 3 hours or until very firm.

In a large microwave-safe measuring cup, melt chocolate chips, stirring until smooth. Reserve ¼ cup chopped candy. Stir remaining candy into chocolate until melted. With a toothpick, dip one frozen cake ball into melted chocolate to coat, gently tapping toothpick on the side of measuring cup to let excess chocolate drip back into cup. Place on waxed paper, remove toothpick and fill in hole with a drop of melted chocolate. Immediately sprinkle top with reserved chopped candy before chocolate sets. Work in small batches, leaving remaining cake balls in the freezer until dipping. Serve cold or at room temperature.

Cheeky

Chocolate Fondue

Ingredients

6 T. heavy whipping cream

1 tsp. grated orange zest

1 C. plus 2 T. semi-sweet chocolate chips

½ tsp. instant coffee granules dissolved in ½ tsp. hot water

2 T. light corn syrup

3 T. **Grand Marnier liqueur**

Dippers: fresh strawberries, green and red apple wedges*, dried pineapple chunks, dried apricots

* Dip sliced apples in lemon juice to prevent browning; drain well.

Directions

In a large glass measuring cup, combine whipping cream and orange zest. Microwave until hot, about 60 seconds. Add chocolate chips and let stand for 1 to 2 minutes to soften; stir to mix. Add coffee and corn syrup; stir until smooth. Whisk in **Grand Marnier**. Transfer mixture to a fondue pot or a glass bowl set over hot water and serve warm with skewers of strawberries, apples, pineapple and apricots for dipping.

Punchy

Peach Fondue

Serves 20

Ingredients

¾ C. heavy whipping cream

1 (12 oz.) pkg. white baking chips

2 (15 oz.) cans peaches, drained, pureed

¼ C. **light rum, white chocolate liqueur** or **peach schnapps**

Dippers: angel food cake cubes, shortbread cookies, meringue cookies, marshmallows, pretzels, ladyfingers

Directions

In a large glass measuring cup, microwave whipping cream until very hot, 1½ to 2 minutes. Add white chips and let stand for 1 to 2 minutes to soften. Whisk until smooth. Stir in peach puree. Whisk in **rum**. Transfer mixture to a fondue pot or a glass bowl set over hot water and serve warm with skewers of angel food cake cubes, shortbread or meringue cookies, marshmallows, pretzels or ladyfingers. Sauce may also be served cold.

Crocked
Vodka
Apples

Ingredients

⅓ C. brown sugar

3 T. chopped dried cherries

2 T. chopped almonds, toasted*

2 T. chopped pecans, toasted*

6 large McIntosh or other baking apples

4 T. butter, divided

½ C. apple cider

½ C. plus 1 T. **apple vodka**, divided

½ C. sugar

½ C. heavy whipping cream

Pinch of salt

Serves 6

Preheat oven to 400°. In a small bowl, stir together brown sugar, cherries, almonds and pecans; set aside. Using a paring knife, core each apple and remove seeds, cutting the hole large enough to hold about 1½ tablespoons of brown sugar mixture without cutting all the way through the bottom of the apple. Place cored apples in a 9 x 13″ baking pan. Fill each apple with about 1½ tablespoons of brown sugar mixture, packing down lightly. Reserve remaining brown sugar mixture. Cut 3 tablespoons butter into six equal pieces and place one piece on top of each apple, pressing down lightly.

Stir together apple cider and ½ cup **apple vodka**; pour into baking dish around apples. Bake for 25 minutes or until apples are just tender, basting apples with liquid every 5 minutes.

Meanwhile, in a small saucepan over medium heat, stir together sugar and 2 tablespoons water. Cook and stir until sugar dissolves. Increase heat to high, bring to a boil and cook until golden brown, stirring constantly. Remove from heat and very slowly stir in whipping cream until well blended. If sauce begins to harden, return saucepan to stove briefly. Add salt and remaining 1 tablespoon butter, stirring until butter melts. Stir in remaining 1 tablespoon **apple vodka**.

Transfer baked apples to serving dishes and pour some of the liquid from the baking dish over each apple. Sprinkle with reserved brown sugar mixture and serve with warm sauce.

* To toast, place almonds and pecans on a baking sheet in a 350° oven for about 10 minutes or until evenly browned, stirring occasionally.

Index